WHAT CAN I DO TODAY?

MAKE A DOLL'S HOUSE

Illustrated by Brian Edwards

Purnell

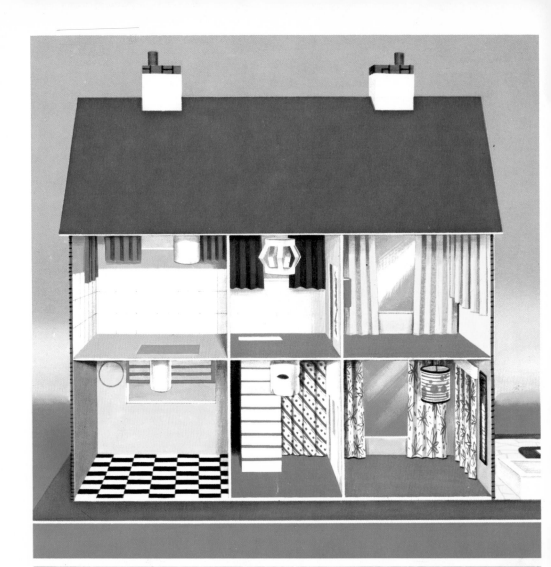

Making the House (Stage 1)

You will need:
Two cardboard boxes 46cm × 32cm × 27cm
Piece of hardboard or
plywood 75cm × 51cm for base
Scissors, glue, Sellotape,
polythene bags
Pencil, penknife,
coloured paints

(Note: Similar shaped but
different sized boxes can be
used. In this case follow
general instructions, but
adjust sizes to fit your
boxes)

Making the House (Stage 1)

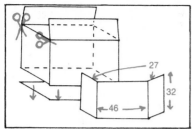

1. Cut and remove top, bottom and back of box one, leaving front and sides. Open out flat.

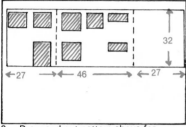

2. Draw and cut pattern above for windows. Turn over and tape pieces of polythene bags over window openings for glass.

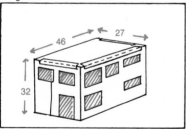

3. Cut two panels, size 27cm × 46cm, from front and back of box two. Fold walls and tape panels on top and bottom.

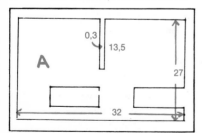

4. Make two pieces as pattern above from the sides of box two. These are for inside walls.

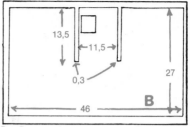

5. Draw and cut out pattern above from the back of box one. This piece divides the house into two storeys.

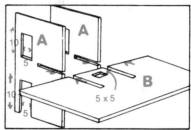

6. Paint all the walls inside and out white at this stage. Slot inside walls A into section B, as shown.

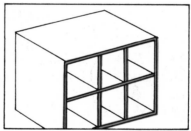

7. Tape or glue this completed section onto the inside of the house to form the rooms.

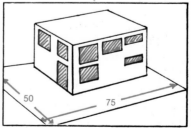

8. Glue the house onto the base in position shown. Now make roof; see separate stage.

Making the Roof (Stage 2)

You will need:

Two pieces of thick cardboard or corrugated board 48cm × 24cm
Two pieces of thick cardboard or corrugated board 20cm × 30cm

Two pieces of thin card 21.5cm × 11.5cm
Two pieces of thin card 2.5cm × 4cm
Tape, glue, scissors, penknife, coloured paints

Making the Roof (Stage 2)

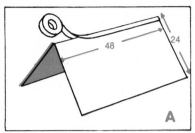

1. Take thick cards 48cm × 24cm and join together with tape. Leave 3mm between to allow pieces to bend easily.

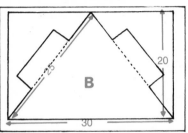

2. Draw 2 sections as above on thick card 20cm × 30cm. Cut and fold as shown. These are for roof supports.

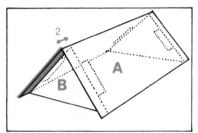

3. Glue roof supports B into roof top A. Leave 2cm overlap at each end of roof.

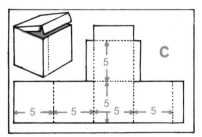

4. Draw and cut 2 sections as above from thin cards 21.5cm × 11.5cm. Fold and glue tabs to make chimney stacks.

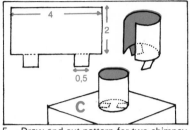

5. Draw and cut pattern for two chimney pots from thin card 4cm × 2.5cm. Roll and glue edge. Glue tabs onto stacks.

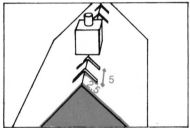

6. Cut a pair of slots 5cm apart and 2.5cm deep at each end of the roof top. Fit chimney stacks into slots.

7. Place the roof on the house.

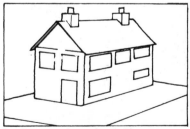

8. Decorate the roof and chimneys with coloured paints to complete the exterior of the house.

Garden Landscape (Stage 3)

You will need:

Coloured paper 11.5cm square
Coloured paper for path
Thin card 20cm × 10cm
Thin card 12.5cm × 10cm
Two cotton reels

Two small twigs
Egg carton lid or paper tray
Glue, scissors, pencil, ruler
Coloured paints

Garden Landscape (Stage 3)

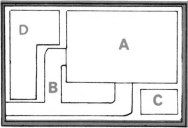

1. Draw out the plan on your base in pencil. A is the house; B path; C patio and D pool.

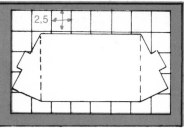

5. Draw and cut paper pattern for canopy over door. Fold and glue over door.

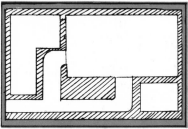

2. Paint the shaded areas green.

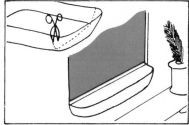

6. Cut an egg carton lid or paper tray to make window box. Glue below window.

3. Cut irregular shapes in grey or brown paper and glue them to the paths.

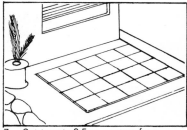

7. Cut twenty 2.5cm squares from 12.5cm × 10cm card. Glue them on the base to make patio (C).

4. Cut and glue on 2 pieces of coloured paper 6cm × 11.5cm from paper 11.5cm square, for front doors. Paint on door knobs.

8. Paint 2 reels white and put them at either side of the front door, with a small twig in each.

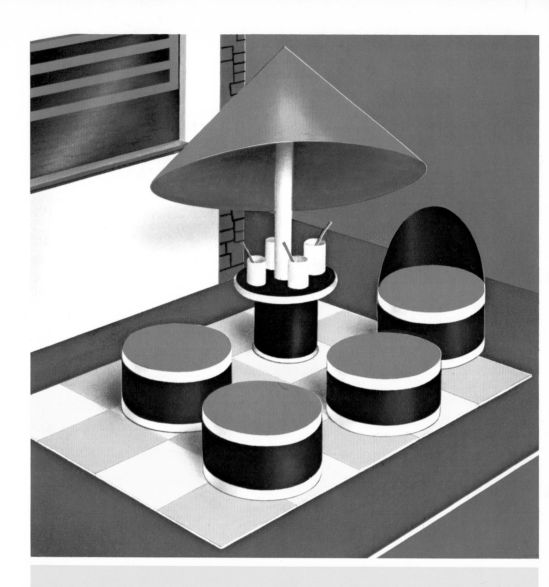

Garden Furniture and Pool (Stage 4)

You will need:

Sheet of thin coloured card
Toilet roll tube
Cotton reel
Lolly stick
Pieces of thin card for sides
of pool: 30cm × 10cm, 20cm × 10cm,
17cm × 10cm, 13cm × 10cm and two
10cm × 10cm

Glue
Pencil, scissors, coloured
paints

Garden Furniture and Pool (Stage 4)

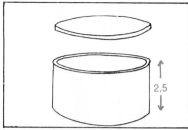

1. Cut four 2.5cm lengths from toilet roll tube. Cut four discs from card to fit the tops and glue into place for chairs.

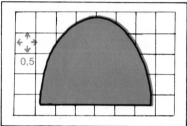

2. Draw and cut pattern for seat back from card and glue to one seat.

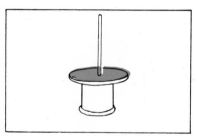

3. For table glue a 4cm disc of card to top of cotton reel. Push the stick through the centre.

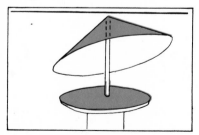

4. Make sunshade from a 11.5cm disc of paper. Cut and glue into cone. Fix on top of stick as shown.

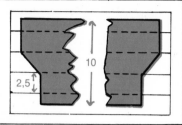

5. Draw and cut out above shapes at each end of the cards for sides of pool. Fold along dotted lines.

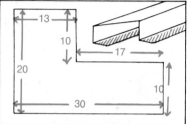

6. Glue into position around pool, following the above plan. Paint bottom of pool blue.

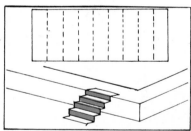

7. Make steps from card 6cm × 2.5cm. Fold at every 6mm as shown and glue into place.

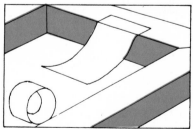

8. Cut two 5cm × 2.5cm strips of card. Curve one for chute and make other into tube for decoration. Glue both to pool.

Lounge Furniture (Stage 5)

You will need:
Egg box carton lid
Thin coloured card
Stiff coloured paper
Tin foil 8cm × 4cm

Scissors, glue, ruler,
coloured paints
Pencil

Lounge Furniture (Stage 5)

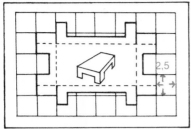

1. Draw pattern for table on card. Cut along solid lines, fold along dotted lines and glue together.

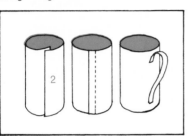

2. Cut a 2.5cm × 2cm piece of card. Glue into a tube for jug. Stick on a thin strip of card for handle.

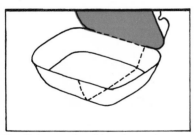

3. Cut an egg box lid as shown, to make couch.

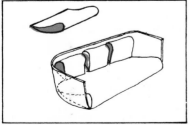

4. Cut and bend squares of paper for cushions. Glue to couch as shown. Use smaller squares for little cushions.

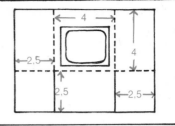

5. Draw pattern above on card for T.V. Cut along solid lines, fold along dotted lines and glue together to make box.

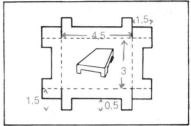

6. Draw and cut pattern for T.V. table from card. Fold along dotted lines and glue together. Decorate with paints.

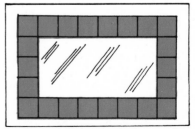

7. Draw and cut patterns for three seats from card. Roll 10cm strips into tubes and glue on cushions and backs.

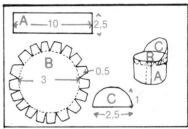

8. Cut card 10cm × 5cm for frame and glue a piece of foil 8cm × 4cm inside to make a mirror. Glue to wall.

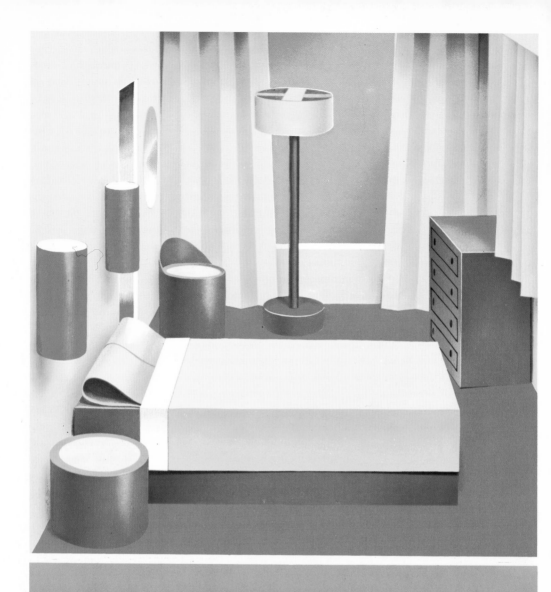

Bedroom Furniture (Stage 6)

You will need:

Stiff coloured paper
Lolly stick
Thin coloured card

Pencil, scissors, ruler
Glue, coloured paints

Bedroom Furniture (Stage 6)

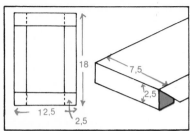

1. Draw and cut pattern for bed from card 18cm × 12.5cm. Fold along lines and glue.

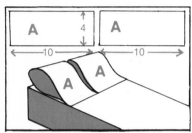

2. Fold 2 pieces of thin card 10cm × 4cm as shown. Glue to top of bed for pillows.

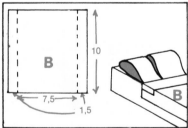

3. Fold piece of paper 10cm × 10.5cm as shown, and glue on bed for bedspread. Add strip of white paper for sheet.

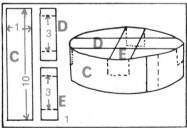

4. Draw and cut paper patterns for lampshade and glue together as shown.

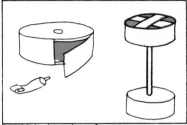

5. Make lamp base from two cardboard discs 4cm diameter and paper strip, as shown. Push stick in base and glue shade on top.

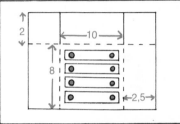

6. Draw and cut card 15cm × 10cm for chest of drawers. Fold along dotted lines and glue. Decorate with paints.

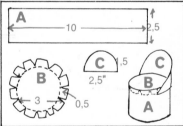

7. Draw and cut patterns for two seats from card. Roll 10cm strips into tubes and glue on cushions and backs.

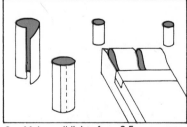

8. Make wall-lights from 2.5cm squares of paper. Roll into tubes and glue to wall above bed.

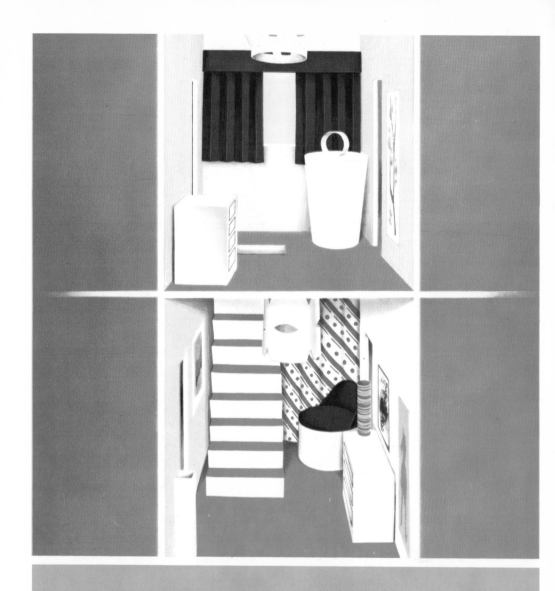

Hall and Landing Furniture (Stage 7)

You will need:
Coloured paper
Thin card

Coloured paints
Scissors, glue, pencil, ruler

Hall and Landing Furniture (Stage 7)

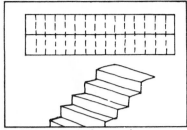

1. Make the stairs from card 27cm × 5cm. Fold on dotted lines as shown.

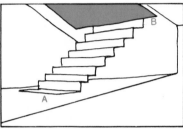

2. Glue one end of the staircase to hall floor and the other end to the opening in the landing floor.

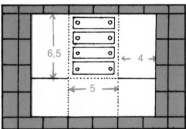

3. Draw and cut pattern for landing chest from card. Fold along dotted lines and glue together. Decorate.

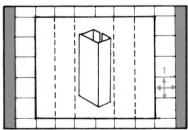

4. Draw and cut pattern for umbrella stand from card 7.5cm × 6.5cm. Fold on dotted lines and glue to wall in hall.

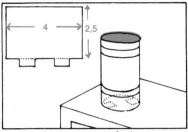

5. Draw and cut pattern for lamp on a 3cm × 4cm piece of paper. Roll and glue as shown. Glue onto hall chest.

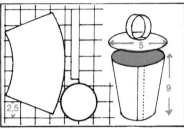

6. Draw and cut pattern for basket from card 20cm × 18cm. Bend and glue. Glue on 5cm diameter disc for lid. Add paper handle.

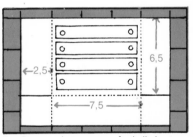

7. Draw and cut pattern for hall chest from card. Fold along dotted lines and glue together. Decorate as shown.

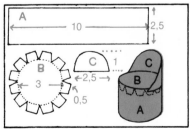

8. Draw and cut pattern for hall chair from card. Roll 10cm strip into tube and glue on cushion and back.

Kitchen Furniture (Stage 8)

You will need:
Thin card
Scissors, pencil, ruler

Glue, coloured paints

Kitchen Furniture (Stage 8)

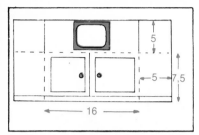

1. Draw and cut pattern above for sink unit from card. Fold along dotted lines.

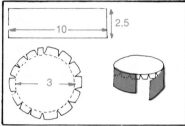

5. Draw pattern for table on card. Cut along solid lines, fold along dotted lines and glue.

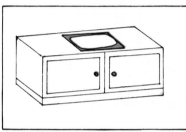

2. Glue together as shown, and decorate with paints. Place in position in kitchen.

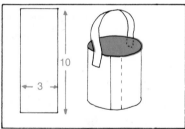

6. Draw and cut pattern for chair from card. Roll 10cm strip into tube and glue on cushion as shown.

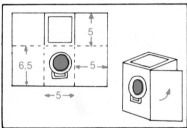

3. Draw and cut pattern above for washing machine from card. Fold along dotted lines and glue together. Decorate as shown.

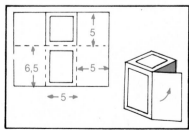

7. Draw and cut pattern for bucket from card. Roll 10cm strip into tube and glue. Add small card strip for handle.

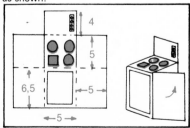

4. Draw and cut pattern for cooker from card. Fold along dotted lines and glue together. Decorate as shown.

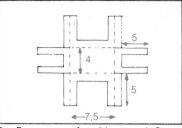

8. Draw and cut pattern for fridge from card. Fold along dotted lines and glue as shown. Decorate with paints.

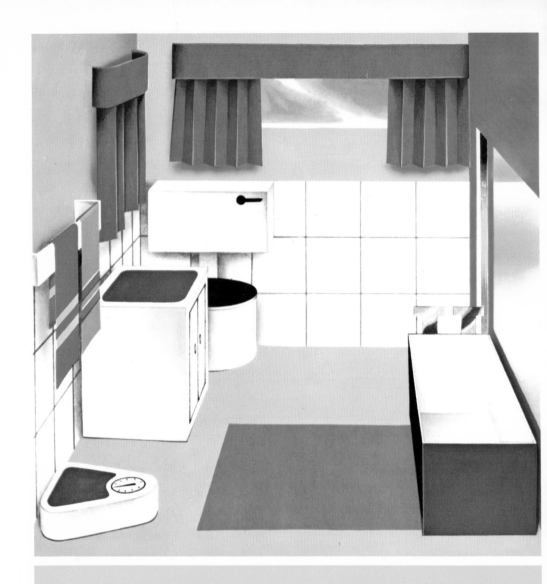

Bathroom Furniture (Stage 9)

You will need:
Thick card 0.6cm × 7.5cm
Thin card
Tin foil
Toilet roll tube

Coloured paper
Scissors, glue, ruler, pencil
Black paint

Bathroom Furniture (Stage 9)

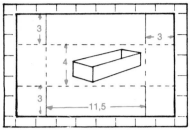

1.   Draw pattern for bath on card 18cm × 10cm. Cut along solid lines, fold along dotted lines and glue together.

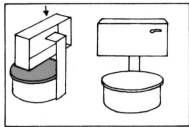

5.   Fold 0.6cm of toilet upright over and glue on cistern as shown.

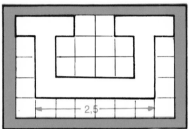

2.   Glue foil onto card 3cm × 2.5cm. Draw and cut pattern above for bath taps from it and glue into position.

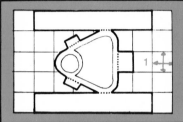

6.   Draw and cut pattern for scales from card 7.5cm × 6.5cm. Fold along dotted lines and glue together. Decorate with paint.

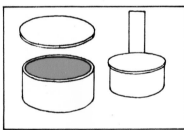

3.   Cut a 2.5cm piece of tube for toilet. Glue a paper disc on the top. Glue 0.6cm × 7.5cm thick card in position shown.

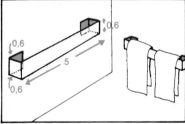

7.   Cut and fold card 7.5cm × 0.6cm for towel rail. Glue to wall. Cut two pieces of paper 5cm × 2cm, fold and hang as shown.

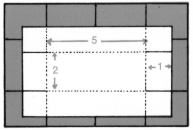

4.   Draw and cut pattern for cistern from card 7.5cm × 4.5cm. Fold on dotted lines and glue together. Paint on handle.

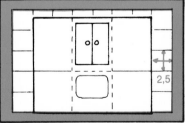

8.   Draw and cut pattern for cupboard from card 15cm × 12.5cm. Fold along dotted lines and glue. Decorate as shown.

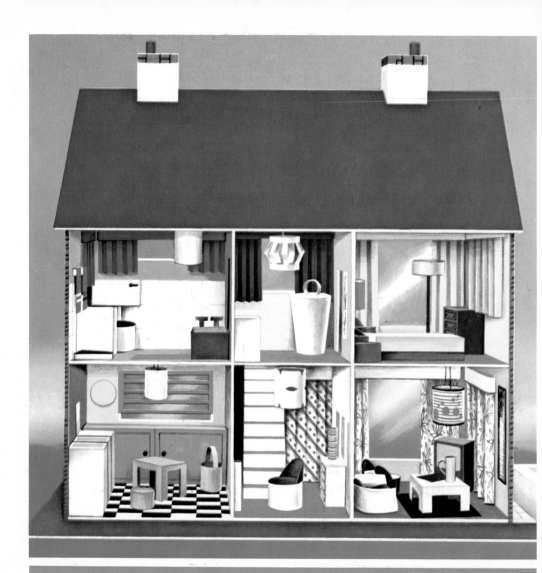

Decorating the Rooms (Stage 10)

You will need:
Thin card
Scissors, glue,
needle and thead

Sellotape
Coloured paper